NO MOAT NO CASTLE

NO MOAT NO CASTLE

poems by
Donald F. Drummond

Alan Swallow: Denver: 1949

Many of these poems have been printed previously in The Hudson Review, Poetry: A Magazine of Verse, and in Poets of the Pacific, an anthology of western poets, edited by Yvor Winters.

CONTENTS

NO MOAT NO CASTLE

ON A BOOK BY JOHN MILTON, ANNOTATED.

Repository where the plane
Of page and line imprison thought
Although the past dies, one foot caught
Within the cloth-lined trap, the stain
Of tortured action must remain.

The stain impels the consequent
Tradition-hungry, over-weight
Pursuer of the fleeing great
To stir the covers of event
Disturbing what the plane had meant

When hot and not benevolent
The words lay dripping on the page
Controlled above by his love and rage
By what had been a cold intent
To suffer with the innocent.

THE FROWARD GULL

The bird has flared his wingtips on the reef,
His beak extended like a whale boat prow;
And individual evil past belief
With caution teeters on the point of Now.
Gulls beyond sudden counting stiffly set
And tack their wings like cutters. In their glide—
The flash of wings above the flash of wet—
Is movement, universal as the tide.

No carrion taints that motion in the air.
No quick reflection lights these crusted eyes:
Upon black reef I shun the knowing stare,
Seeking the separate principle which flies:
Between this only and these many birds
Lies ancient paradox escaping words.

FIVE TIMES ZERO

In Rock Springs, snow beside the tracks
Lies grey from locomotive smoke;
The quick cold hems the yellow shacks
And covers that worn oxen yoke

Which lay across two labored necks,
Before the yellow shacks were built
That felt the quick cold in the flex
Of muscle over mud and silt

Where arrowheads of quartsite lay
Before the oxen blundered by,
Containing cold each winter day
Since wind had blown the red blood dry

And fleshless lay the antelope
On hills which bore the absolute
Of absent warmth, which changed their slope
Changed yoke and oxen and the brute

Who shot the arrowhead with hope
And knew the hope die with its fall:
The cold endures the death of each,
Usurps the primacy of all,
Denies the fumbling power of speech.

MEMORIAL AFTER A YEAR

Because dominion is not dead
And you are dead who loved it least,
Your common yet uncommon head
Must serve as scapegoat at this feast

Where all the burdens of your years
With steady courage fairly met
Serve no examples to your peers
Who have not quit invective yet.

Yet this slow ebbing tide shall rise
And wash again upon this coast,
That crippled strength outwear the lies,
And you shall stand above this host

Who crawl above your vanished length
And gain their stature from your breath:
Our common gain grew from your strength,
Our common loss stems from your death.

LONG TERM PROPHECY

Beyond the Red Sea rose a plain
Where Moses saw the heathen slain
He stood above them with the Rod
Outthrust, a man commanding God;
His arms drooped and the banners trailed,
The hosts of Amalek prevailed,
He raised his arms, the heathen fled
Across a desert wet and red.

But for the mind's drift is no shore
No reef of coral breaks the floor
Of ocean where that coral grew
Before the atom broke in two:
Hallucination by degrees
Has blown the palm fronds from the trees,
Hallucination measured by
Geiger counters in the sky:

No lesser magic, these alarms
Than from old Moses' trembling arms,
Since when his elbows quake we feel
Rapid encroachment of the real
Beyond our measured senses, know
Why law and magic make it grow:
Till with the foetus flames the rake,
Till with the woman burns the snake.

And in our general order then
Is neither man nor nitrogen,
And where the Geiger counters range
Destruction synonyms with change:
And rotting protoplasm's smell
Affords a preview into hell
Where ancient Moses, stiff and sore
Can hold out aching arms no more.

EPITAPH FOR A RENO WOMAN

(For it is easier for a camel to go through a needle's eye, than for a rich man to enter into the kingdom of God

St. Luke 18:25)

A pound of flesh, a pound of gold,
Are each my life, and each is old;
And neither worth the other's loss:
The heart needs gold to give it gloss
And no gold gleams without the Heart:
In each the other's counterpart.
And though rich women force that gate
They do not bear my double weight.

The great she-camel's stomachs swell:
She trots on madly by to hell.
And though I diet endlessly
My mind has fixed the width of me;
The narrow gate called Needle's Eye,
Exacts its penance, though I die:
For heaven gained, sans gold or touch
For two-humped beasts is not worth much.

CAUTION

Beware Aristotelian man,
Baal's bloody idols do not fall
By categories to your scan
And often tumble not at all.

Your catalog may not include
Twin rattlesnakes entwined below
A crown of porphyry: the crude
And polished art of Tezcuco.

The grim Dacotah waste of soul
Before a deer trapped in a pit
Writes nothing on your careful scroll,
Though death and madness come of it:

Empirical and evident
Are strength and motion, form and size:
None saw, when Samson's back was bent,
Intention in his mangled eyes.

TIME AT TIMBERLINE

Within this gray substantial rock
In changeless process heat and cold
Shear off the planes which interlock
Into a pyramidal mold:
Describe a mountain on a base
Whirling in speculative space.

Below the rock-slide lies this earth
These particles of granite pan,
Providing victual for the birth
Of vegetable into man:
The fall of fragments like his bone
Is not determined by the stone.

The glint of quartz along the cleft
Of granite, when the pieces fall
Provides a standard for the deft
Repair of cliff-face, that is all
Progression into utter doom
And changeless space within his tomb.

STATEMENT FOR A SUN DANCE

The bones of chiefs, diminished dread
In bare Nebraska dance at dawn,
Not all the awkward chants are said
Nor all the drum beat rituals gone.

Nor from the eagle's pole descends
The god who parcels out the storm
His immobility transcends
The dancer frozen in his form.

Nor from those eagle talons drip
The essence of his blood or bone:
And at the frozen dancer's hip
The knife succeeds the hammered stone.

For when the sun-pipes blow, we see
The empty god-head on a pole,
Nor can the willow branches be
A sign of universal soul.

No ancient figure-writing rests
Beneath the academic scan,
No sandstone metaphysic dressed
With the deportment of a man.

The rhetoric of Crazy Horse
Is gone without inscription there.
Forgotten signet of that force
Are senseless feathers stuck in hair.

18

TO HART CRANE

Oh lost pariah of a fair Cathay,
The Bridge extended to a lunar pole
Becomes a lost boy drifting in the sea,
Lunatic, leperous, and free.

The final immobility descends
To freeze your heart's blood in a proper hell
Distinct from heaven by the reason's act;
Yet your great dissolution is a fact

No Bridge affirms: the great surrender made
To shroud the intellect which grew afraid,
Trembling and helpless while this ageless sea
Devoured the mortal, held the mystery.

SCIENTIST ON A PODIUM

(A lecture on the empiric method)

The academic vision interferes
Between the lectern and the object man;
Hallucination predicates the van
Of knowledge lodged between his pointed ears.

The vision grows as pride becomes remote:
The student falters as the symbols fall
In tongued remonstrance at the end of all
In each beginning, from that noble throat.

Engraving on that ample brain foretells
Expanse of growth beyond the primate known:
Although his bone may break like human bone,
An altered order functions in those cells

Which speed the act, suspend the act, or fall
Between the actor and the absolute,
Between the music and the perfect flute
Piped once at Hamlin-town beyond the wall.

The academic vision shows the pride
Of pride discarded for the sake of truth:
Discarded is the constancy of Ruth,
Discarded is the piercing of the side.

ANTHROPOMORPHISM

The thundering hammer of the ape
Against his chest in mating season,
Obtrudes its manner on the shape
Of individual man, a treason

Not to be endured by some,
Who castigate the young gorilla
Because he owns an off-set thumb,
And sometimes likes his sasparilla.

Ape-like, offended by the mock
Of what became a category
Designed to show a common stock,
And to define a common story,

The reason-twisting brute rebels,
Extracting from the intellectual,
The eye which sees, the nose which smells,
The act which makes a thought effectual.

THE BLOOD OF THE LAMB

The damp wool of the ewe protects the lamb
Which nurses on her lee side in the storm,
The urgent head pressed sharply to its dam
Escapes the winter and explains the norm
Of metabolic process gressed in time,
The balanced heat and cold, the mean of law,
The principle of motion in the lime,
Once ewe and lamb crouched numbly in a draw.

Mother to mother yields, the snow returns:
So each the other, absolute in change:
The surge of seasons and the swell of birth
Give meaning to a lamb upon the range,
Nudging the rank wool where the udder churns
The causal liquid which repairs the earth.

INTUITIVE ESSENTIAL

For one sign granted in the weltering night
Which is this trap of flesh wherein I fall,
Self-poisoner and poisoned, let me find
Rune or old symbol, any mark of faith
By which I learn that Lazarus' recall
Has altered one condition of his frame.

Within this trap of flesh wherein I move
Color and cold are kept, the flashing mind
Repairs its tentacles: my ears, my eyes
Repeat the faithful construct and intent
Of what is there to see: remaining blind
To what moves Lazarus behind the stone.

Self-poisoner and poisoned, let me find
Once in the dusk of timber on this height
The spring of motion and the spark of sound
Not in the principle, but in the man:
Know the immortal sense, the hurrying flight
Of universal color on a nerve.

THE MEEK SHALL INHERIT

The meek inherit what we do not know
Nor do the meek know that which they inherit;
But after every snow cloud comes the snow,
And after every mouse a hungry ferret:
The action in the form the actor's show—
The meek inherit what, we do not know.

A pound of weight, a quart of size, a flow
Of oboe notes, a noose below a gibbet:
Each in itself seems what the measures show,
An opium dream an act which dreams prohibit.
Within the form the meaning's here below:
A pound of weight, a quart of size, a blow.

Upon these cortices the flickers grow,
The complex of the mind becomes remote.
And simple meekness puzzled by the show—
Excess of judgment from the nervous throat—
In desperation sheds tomorrow's woe,
Nor do the meek inherit what we know.

SONG FOR A VIOLENT CALIFORNIA CITY

Spreading like a new disease
Beneath the eucalyptus trees
Is rank profusion and the smell
Of dead geraniums whose leaves
Rot within the stagnant well.

The foreign mountaineer believes
This growth, perverted with the ease
Of growing, turns upon its own,
And strikes the plant down with the shoot
That riotous plant had gaily sown.

Untwist the tangles of the root
Which winds around my mountain boot.
In tropic growth, the fiber's lost
Which twisted mountain pine has grown,
And placed at everlasting cost
In each infrequent cone.

THE BIGGEST LITTLE CITY

The sterile prompting of the age
To flee the quick and heed the dead,
The whimpering of sense outrage
By the wan commerce of the bed

Imperils all this waste of stone,
This talkless tavern of a town,
Where love equates the fleshy groan
Of whore and madman bedded down:

And on their faces lies no dread
Of wrath withheld nor evil known,
The grinning lines about each head
Have sunk into the bone.

TO MY FATHER

The strong grow stronger in their faith
And from their strength their faith grows strong.
And you who fastened on a wraith
Which moved John Wesley were not wrong

To fix your being to that rock
From which the purest water flowed,
Allying pity to the stock
Whom Calvin fired into a goad

Which pricked old kings and cardinals
To fury, and whose faith subdued
The Plymouth winter, and the calls
Of flesh which tore the multitude,

Who built a solitary state
Upon the bare Laurentian soil,
Who looked on slothfulness with hate
That moment they were hating toil.

You were not wrong to scorn the man
Who scorning, turned the other cheek,
Nor with your grave religious scan
To seek the best which best men seek.

And you may challenge, not condemn
The risk each generation runs:
That faith from which your being stems
Prove insubstantial to your sons.

GENERATION OF INTENTION

The elder boy I do not know:
  The dark eyes by the sun embossed
Record eight years, the structures grow—
  Who sees most clearly, most has lost.

The infant wailing in the dark,
  The nightmare of the early bed,
I hear no more; where is the mark
  They fastened in his eager head?

The tiny fingers grasped at Time
  Like a damp ring above a crib,
The scar is buried in the slime
  Where Adam lost another rib,

Where graying Priam heard the shout
  When Hector fell, or where the king
Found Absalom below the knout
  Of tangled hair. To name the thing

Which makes remote the root and flower,
  Sustaining variation won—
To name it Time arrests no hour,
  Grants me no boon to know my son.

THE WEDDING RING

The documented union of these hands
Authority has blessed with pomp refined
By countless unions; through the golden bands
The fingers slip, the flickering nervous kind,
The hardened digits of the dumb and slow
Suborned by ecstasy, the cynic's stem
Of cultivated scorn extended here
In genuflection to the law of man.

So to this altar came the scented head
Of Clytemnestra and her black-browed Greek,
Of Desdemona when the lacy bed
Extended generation to the meek,
Of Jezabel when Ahab knew his strength
Was born of God, and at her garment's hem,
Dissolved like salt; before they grew in fear—
Before the poison of the Will began.

THE ENDLESS ERROR

Jenghiz upon the mountains white and high
Saw near a cliff a tiny frozen bird,
Then raised his sword and watched the Moslems die
Till not a single bloody body stirred.
Elizabeth spoke a poison-arrowed word
And Mary died beneath the headsman's hand,
And Pilate shunned the evidence he heard
To raise a Cross which shadowed Holy Land:

These by the Scorpion's touch, the queer Unplanned,
These by the headsman, governor, or Khan.
And no God makes the mighty understand
Why all of Satan's songs are undersung.
No Mercy tempers what the silence sheds
Upon the mighty in their lonely beds.

NOEL

Not sacred that a woman bore a king,
No miracle to see the molten star,
Not that thin shepherds heard great voices sing,
Nor wise men riding in an armored car,
Is the significant, the wide event,
The century-nursed obsession of each heart
Which feeds upon its own divine portent:
Of that it cherishes, itself a part;

Peace on the earth, unpeaceful earth, oh peace,
From each man in his heart to each man met—
Unpledged communicants—for each release,
A truce among the blood and tears and sweat;
From David's city to the lonely hill
Only a little time, and yet goodwill.

And Claudius Nero laughing in his cage
No more, nor in the threatening gloom
Of blacked-out cities, hear the motors roar
Over the tension of the quivering room,
For this one season, we imagine sheep
Upon the darkening hills, like any shepherd;
Where we lie down to strange and fearless sleep
Unmindful of the thin, longwhiskered leopard.

For in a mind, acts are their own intent,
And this the time of catholic intention
When mercy is a week-end leave to Ghent
Parade-rest after standing at attention.
From David's city to the lonely hill
Only a little time, and yet goodwill.

Mary, the mother, lying in the shed
Heard the faint birth-cry: felt that men were flesh,
Were blood and bone and lying in a bed,
Were time and hope and trouble in a mesh.
But gallant too were men: unsimple, able,
Like Solomon adept at splitting hairs,
At carving up a baby on a table,
At mounting golden flights of Jacob's stairs.

So like her love—stronger in its season—
When the old year is hard upon its ends,
Over the fallacies of man's unreason
The warmth of mangers and of stars descends,
Only a little time, and yet goodwill
From David's city to Golgotha's hill.

PRIMITIVE

Upon the hornblende in the deep cave dance
   Figures scratched in lead;
The dancing bodies leap above a lance
   Inscribed in oxide red,
Which eye and nerve defined upon the wall,
   An allegory grown
Like that of Socrates to shackle All
   Into condensed unknown.
These leaped above the buried when the first
   Ring-necked pheasant quill
Interpreted the dancing heathens' thirst
   With ink-horne pedant's thrill—
Described the ever-dancing breasted throng
   By one slim mark set down,
And wrote a single dance and single song
   Within a single noun:
The figures' movement absolutely kept
   To prison our adept,
And when the dance gained scripture by that act
   Dance became artifact.

HOW SLEEP THE BRAVE

(An expedition of school girls to the Hall of Fame.)

Although the words of men suffice
To grant them wise and name them great,
To make them heroes of the state
And fix their place in Paradise,

Although the noble words are said
And statues hammered, bronze or stone,
No memory of the perished tone
Contemns the bronzes of these dead,

Beneath that vast invested room
Where the great leaves of history fall
The human memory comes to call
Uncritical before the tomb,

And great grandchildren of the strong
Who fell at Breed's without a name
On tiptoe tread the Hall of Fame
Before the bust of Huey Long.

HEDONIC TO HELEN

Of many Helens, one of Troy
Gave pleasure to a smiling boy;
Of many virtues, one she lost
Exacted a tremendous cost
Of blood and armies, men and gold:
What Helen gained is never told.

THE BIOLOGY OF SIN

No matter what the adder said
In that great sea of bloom,
Already fixed in Adam's head
Was one small knot of doom.

And though the tower of Babel fell
Destroyed rung by rung,
Each man his individual hell
Carried in his tongue.

THE ENIGMA OF EVELYN

To Evelyn the world was like a man:
Unjust and frivolous and vainly proud,
Bound to her wishes, poised before her fan,
Viewed incompletely, like a summer cloud.
So small her world, so endlessly complex
Her minute study of what seemed pure whim,
Designed to puzzle and confuse her sex,
She thought it better to dispense with him.

DEAD WIFE

The prescient weather came, blue sage and snow
Were gathered in the wet drift of the fog,
And seven ring-necked pheasants in a row
Patrolled their cat-tail hospice down the bog.
Where pheasants hid, I saw above a stock
Of polished oak, sleep-risen from the mist,
Her slanted eyes alive, and dead as rock—
The fog-damp lips my hunting lips had kissed.

Shadows reached the shadows pressed on shadows
Where pheasants walk within the reed's protection:
This phantom came to me across the meadows
Gun-laden, slanting smiles in my direction
From long ago, when with this aging dog
We sought no pheasant and there was no fog.

COMPLAINT TO A PRINCE

This woman here, your worship, much desired
Has worn upon her head a crown of snakes.
Her breasts are metal-shielded, chained and wired
Upon her hips a belt which Vulcan makes.
Her glance, you note, is open, her brow clear;
Red wine her mouth, a perfect couplet, thighs.
Perfection basely false like those false tears
Which even now are darkening her eyes.

How many wars, Sire, from the heathen won
By such poor men as I have sequels here:
The decorate chest debased for gossips' fun
And heroes crying in their consorts' beer.
The grave ideas lost or laid to rest
Upon the rounded wanton's purchased breast.

THE WORD WAS WITH GOD

The Word is framework where the Thing
    Finds boundaries, but the neatest sin
Applies the word to weave a ring
    Where nothing may be bounded in

Or bounded out, the Spanish lord
    Converts the windmill into wind,
But no less graciously, the board
    Of grey directors, neatly pinned

By maps and charts, afford a glance
    At so much coal upon the wall
Or elevators crammed with chance
    And Kansas wheat. The pages fall

While grain is piled high in burlap sacks
    And each director drips with sweat
The Thing discovers what it lacks
    That words have not discovered yet.

TO INFANT SON AND
INFANT DAUGHTER

Small girl and boy,
Between you each
Dark glances serve
For wider speech,
Defining both the eye and nerve.

Alert each head:
The neck-bones slant
The curious brain
With can or can't
Anticipating joy or pain.

I charge my mind;
This bleak defeat
Of sure and wild
No longer sweet,
With pity for each child.

Blood of my blood:
My father lies
Below my head;
His aging eyes
Are pitiful instead,

As you shall lie
Upon this floor
And looking back
See me no more—
Your black eyes seeking black.

ATHENA LEMNIA

Beneath the idol grew the man:
Implicit in the fashioned scan
Of chiseled eye, her beauty grew
Into the moving shapes he knew.

Into the thought that plagued his head
He drew serenity instead
Of violence for her passion strained
All of the bonds which stone contained,

And yet admitted, so his mind
Grew in the sufferance of his kind.
Hers the contrivance, he, contrived
A renaissance toward which he strived

But which escaped him into stone
While he retained his changing bone.
Stone shall crumble, gods depart
Though no new idol claim his heart.

BELOW THE BELT

To Allen Tate:

I offer up a hymn to Allen Tate,
The goated Mr. Pope, grim love and hate,
And all the meter which I cannot scan
As well as all the meter which I can.

To T. S. Eliot:

Between the violets where the Virgin walks
Lies Mr. Sweeney caught in violet stalks.

To Yvor Winters:

The chiseled good which Yvor Winters turns
Between his fingers makes him hard to please,
And though his critics often die from burns,
His friends as often freeze.

To J. V. Cunningham:

To Mr. J. V. Cunningham
The poison of his epigram,
And if no poison let there be
Jest and youthful jollity.

To Kenneth Patchen:

The whisper which becomes an awful scream
May be esteemed by others; I esteem
The whispered whisper, and the screaming scream.

THE CINDER OF MONTEZUMA

I

For two weeks he had watched the slender trout.
Each morning when the sun had topped the cliff
He slammed the cabin door and ran the path
Pell mell and panting to the pool below.
Beneath the hornblende ledge the water swirled
Over the granite gravel, and the sun
Spilt fragmentary light, acute and green.
Within this light the phantom moved below
The geometric surface. On the rock
Flat on his belly lay the waiting boy.
Upon the surface of the stream a fly
Fell to the water, and a shadow moved
Faster than eyes move; the green water broke,
Erupted like a fountain; the red sides
Flashed in the sun, glimmered within the eye,
And drowned within the water as they shone.
His heart beat hard; his long exhaling breath
Matched the widening circles of the leap.
Here was the king of trout, and reassured
The boy rolled over and soaked up the sun.
The king of fish remained within the pool.
Under the water lay the jutted jaw,
The wicked calculation of the head
Designed for deadly movement, and the soft

Flurry of fins, deceptive in their power,
Crafty, vicious, and omnipotent
Within the swirl of water where he moved.

The sun moved up the sky, and still he lay
Back to the rock. A shadow moved across
His upturned face, and as he turned his head
He saw his father holding rod and reel
And staring at the pool. He raised himself
Explosively as if to hide some shame
Defined between them in the pool below.
"I'm going to try him now," his father said.
The boy looked down and turned his face away.
Carefully the father flexed the rod:
The arced line straightened and the fly described
The human imitation of the flight
Of May-flies over water, patterned curve,
In which he moved again, the water broke:
Fury burned the silk line through the guides.
The rod trembled and bent, the fish began
To fight the nagging pressure at his jaw.
Describing circles in a widening ring
The line tore through the water, and the man
Frowning with tension, fed the constant force,
Gentle, compelling, ruthless, and designed.
The fish broke water once, the agony
Of bursting gill sacs shown in straining lines
Above the water, dissipated strength
Lost in the flurry of his furious wake.
The circles were described more slowly now,
Fatigue decayed the frame, the fish obeyed.

Gently, slowly, sliding on his side,
His rainbow banner open to the air
The king lay netted.

                                        Balanced by the pool
The man held up the net. "Take him," he said.
The boy obeyed. Upon his face the shock
Tightened the skin. Within the bulging strings
The giant rainbow lay and beat his gills.
Then he remembered pools of fish within
The covers of his father's book, where boys
Wandered in formal gardens, spirits lulled
By balanced motion of the trembling fins
Poised in the water, and the Spanish men
Awed by the wonder of those living pools
All in a moment like the captive fish
Were captured by their movement in the sun,
And who had vanquished, who was vanquished known
Neither by sword nor horsemen nor by strength
Of arm nor armour, but by trembling fins.
The father watched the boy who watched the fish.
He saw the eyelids tremble and he knew.
"Ageless the conqueror," he thought, "And now
Comes age before its time, to boys before
The fish grows still." He dropped his arm
Upon the narrow shoulders and they stood
Each for the other's comfort, side by side.

II

He thought, "While youth remains—" the hyphen grew,
Became caesura, and returned to thought.
The hanging clause defined itself in time:
Became a clock's face where the hands had stopped.

The hands had stopped before the sleek grew rod
Tubbed on the fan-tail swung her gaping nose
To fire at space. The monstrous gun became
One force in one equation while the sea
Sustained the mean of motion, grey and great
Complex for which the computations grew.
Within this motion all his dead went home;
His sense grew sick; the flat taste on his tongue
Revealed his memory's substance: thirty years. . . .

Odysseus while riding through the mist
In ceaseless motion on this iron burr
Quite suddenly has heard the tale break off;
Has heard the sirens wailing close aboard.
Beneath the denim shirt the stomach turns
Less at the old sea's motion than this new
Decline of muscled fiber on the frame,
The anguish of the waist line slacking large.
Odysseus off the lotus island hears
The thunder of the guns beyond the surf:
Penelope has waited, let the sea
Clock all its rollers, when the aging gull
Returns to shore the gull falls. Let it be.

The gull has tossed the shell case to the sea;

Performed the ritual of the five-inch piece
And washed the taste of lotus from his mouth:
Anticipating suddenly the sag
Below her breasts, the drying facial skin,
The mottling of her thighs before the cold.
Between his eyes the frown ascends. The clause
Frowns in his mind. The sudden shift
From youth to not youth has not calmed the sea.
The masts lean over like an old man's stick
As he leans with them welcoming the fog.

III

Beyond the creek bed lay a bank of sand
Choke cherry brush had shaded from the sun.
Here beneath spread elbows he had held
The great recorded "Conquest" of the blind
Dry-witted Prescott, who had drawn it all:
Shaped and erected pyramidal towers,
Hewn down the live-oak forests on the hills,
And watched the king's sons perish in the lake.
Mexico!
              The adolescent dream land where the brave
Devoured the brave, before the dream became
Lost in the fact of driving home the cows.

The man fell to the sand. His elbows spread
To hold his chin. In this same stream
A fish had shown the end. And now he knew,
Remembering Prescott, where the Will began.
Before his eyes in this dear place there grew

The fabled end: the prince, who watched the fish
Play in the terraced garden in blue pools,
Had gone down to the wars and won them all,
Even the last one, when the temples fell.
"Begin again," he thought, "begin again."
High-pitched the quavering priest's voice split the air:
A roar prolonged and violent broke against
The carven steps, reflected from the stone
Like sun on Aztec water, with that noise
Their terror and tradition grew together
Into the mass mind, and each will became
A drop of water with its boundaries lost
In channeled movement down an ancient street.
The red heart dripped and shuddered in his hand.
The roar diffused, quieted. A cloud
Darkened the June blaze and the hot wind died.
The up-turned mouths were hushed. The high
                              priests' shout
Shot out above them darkening their eyes,
"Huitzilopotchi's hunger must be fed!"
The outthrust arms enforced hysteria
On the brown mass below. Priest food!
Red blood of living hearts, the dying flesh
Of Tlasclan muscle for their minds to chew!
The hot breeze slipped again down temple steps
Bearing the smell of death, last summer's death:
Yucatan blood interred with Tlasclan's smell—
The hot and acrid mixed with slow decay
Vanished in Time, charged with the total deed.
Bright turquoise nose-rings lifted in the crowd;
The sleeping beast of being like a stream

Breaking an earth dam at the weakest clod
Flowed to the palace wall, eddied about
The brazen gates. Stamping and screaming men
Began to move. Upon the wall above
The chain-mail glittered bright below the beards:
"Andale! Andale!" grinning Spaniards mocked
The crush of brilliant Indians in the square.

Suddenly, above the highest gate
A figure grew, held up a wounded arm
Bound with white cotton; all the fury hushed
At one quick motion. His uncovered head
Seemed tall beyond them all. The June breeze blew
Ringlets from his ears, the whitened mail
Glanced in the sunlight like Castilian sun
Definitive and thin. The short beard fell
Black as goat hair hiding cynic lips.
The signal arm descended. Breathless men,
Their bellies tight with nervous dread suspend
In the fixed image of one time all thought.
These willed to wait; in waiting lay all choice;
All hope was fixed beyond the upraised arm.
Beside the Spaniard then the King appeared
Rising above the wall. Beside Cortez
The blazing headdress-feathering proclaimed
The son of god, the legend and the power.
Banded upon his arms the beaten gold,
Hammered to fit tradition without whim
Of artisan and ruler, burned that mark.
The hard left shoulder bared the pride of kings,
The other bore the textiled blue of gods.

What had been sound withheld became
The total silence of the deafened man
After the roar of the cannon. Montezuma—
Gravest of grave men—stood before them all.

The sound of feather brushed against a comb
Became a sovereign's voice. "Men of Tenochitlan!
We are not gods to change the will of gods!
To stop an avalanche an upraised arm
Is less than milkweed down. We are suborned
By our own nature, by the mind which reads
Portents and omens in the common act.
The prophecy of Quixacoatl, harvest's god
Bespoke return when his great back
Turned eastward to the sea, when from his steps
We watched the sun ascend the morning sky.
Return! Perhaps the gods accomplish. We are here!
We are men only, galley-slaves to time.
Memory to teach us what we might have been
Defends us only from remembered things:
Defends no man from destiny, from time,
From flowing water nor the knives of priests.
I have been symbol to you of the force
Which memory feeds. Tradition's spur!
And here that paradox of symbols stands:
Force that directs you, force that unites you,
Force that appends you, broken, goaded, torn
By the same symbol, by that broken spur;
Caught by the force that feeds my very power.
What are the creatures on this parapet?
Had they been men—the Aztec power defers

To no man's power—then I had seen them all
Racked with the skulls along the temple wall."

A single sound cast up, then capped and rolled
Like surf across a reef, subsided, fell
As Montezuma raised a banded arm.
His eyes flashed once and dulled again. He turned
And met the Spaniard's look. He saw the smile
Tighten the bearded lips. "The fate of kings,"
He thought, "The fate of kings is this:
That kings may alter only what they see
And see too little and too much of men,
Too little and too much of gods. They fear
The end of kings which end the men and gods.
Because they cannot see them all they fear:
Fall prey to action's principle. They act
Beyond the time of action, fail to act
When action's needed and they fall from this.
Fear beyond death's an attribute which spreads
Over the grave to childish heads who lean
On the idea mind, on the detached intent.
These heads below me made my laughter warm,
Their hunger made me weep, their love bestowed
That little wisdom which my reign pretends.
Lost! Lost! confused, betrayed, and lost!
King and commanded equally distraught.
But for these simple, how much more destroyed:
Sleep without rest, laughter without mind,
Fury without direction, they reach up
To touch the one sustaining power they knew.

"Children," he cried, "Men of Tenochitlan,
Go to your homes, go peacefully to toil.
Priests to your altars, offer up the prayer
For Montezuma: for the end of War!"

He did not feel the black obsidian piece
Against his temple, hear the roar break through,
The great wall shatter and the Cross fall down.
Before his failing eyes only he saw
The bleak and sudden Spanish smile grow thin:
He thought, "Another calendar to be revised!"
He saw the bitter knowledge light the blue
Hispanian eyes. He read their fear grow fixed:
"In the Beginning," he thought, "in the Beginning!"

*

Oddyseus return! The peacock's screaming
Shatters the quiet garden of my love,
Impelled by neither yearning nor intent,
But screaming, screaming always in the garden.

The New Poetry Series

Of this book, five hundred copies
have been printed by Alan Swallow.
The paper is Dresden Pamphlet,
and the types are hand set Caslon
and Linotype Baskerville.